Published By Nicholas Thompson

@ Edward Mix

Low-carb Diet and Smart Snacking: Low-carb Eating for

Long-term Health and Heart Health Benefits

ISBN 978-87-94477-17-8

TABLE OF CONTENTS

Sweet Potato Lasagna

INGREDIENTS:

- 2 tablespoons of olive oil

- Parsley (chopped)

- 3 potatoes (sliced)

- 1 medium onion (chopped)

- 16 oz. of ricotta cheese

- 5 oz. of spinach

- 1 ½ cups of mozzarella cheese (shredded)

- 1 teaspoon of oregano (dried)

- Kosher salt

- 1 lb. of Italian sausage (without casings and sweet)

- 2 cloves of garlic (diced)

- 2 cups of marinara sauce

- ¾ cup of Parmesan cheese (grated)

- 1 large egg

- Black pepper powder

Directions:

1. Preheat the oven to 375°F (190°C).

2. In a pan, heat oil over medium heat.

3. Add the diced onion to the pan and cook for about 5 minutes until softened.

4. Add the minced garlic to the pan and cook for 1 minute until fragrant.

5. Add the sausage to the pan, breaking it up with a spoon or spatula, and cook until the pink color disappears. Sprinkle it with salt and black pepper.

6. Pour the marinara sauce into the pan and reduce the heat to simmer. Let it cook for 5 minutes.

7. Add the fresh spinach to the pan and cook until it wilts and becomes soft. Remove from heat.

8. In a bowl, whisk together the egg, 1/2 cup of grated Parmesan cheese, ricotta cheese, dried oregano, salt, and black pepper.

9. Grease a baking pan with cooking oil.

10. Spread a layer of the marinara and sausage mixture evenly on the bottom of the baking pan.

11. Place a layer of thinly sliced sweet potatoes on top of the marinara mixture.

12. Spread a layer of the ricotta mixture over the sweet potatoes.

13. Repeat steps 10-12 to create two more layers of marinara, sweet potatoes, and ricotta mixture.

14. Sprinkle shredded mozzarella cheese and the remaining grated Parmesan cheese on top.

15. Cover the baking pan with aluminum foil and bake in the preheated oven for 45 minutes.

16. Remove the foil and continue baking for an additional 15 minutes, or until the sweet potatoes are tender and the cheese is golden and bubbly.

17. Remove from the oven and garnish with fresh parsley.

Garlic Parmesan Oodles

INGREDIENTS:

- 2 cloves of garlic (diced)

- 2 teaspoons of parmesan cheese (grated)

- ¼ teaspoons of parsley (dried)

- Parsley (chopped)

- 1 zucchini

- ¾ tablespoons of olive oil

- ¼ teaspoons of paprika

- Black pepper powder

- Kosher salt

Directions:

1. Preheat the oven to 400°F (200°C).

2. Line a baking pan with foil paper for easy cleanup.

3. Using a spiralizer or a vegetable peeler, cut the zucchini into spirals or thin strips resembling noodles.

4. In a bowl, combine the zoodles, paprika, chopped parsley, minced garlic, olive oil, salt, and black pepper. Mix well, ensuring that the zoodles are coated with the seasonings and oil.

5. Transfer the seasoned zoodles to the prepared baking pan, spreading them out evenly.

6. Bake in the preheated oven for about 10 minutes, or until the zoodles are tender and slightly softened. Be careful not to overcook them, as they can become mushy.

7. Remove the zoodles from the oven and sprinkle the grated Parmesan cheese over the top while they are still hot. The residual heat will help melt the cheese slightly.

8. Garnish with additional chopped parsley for added freshness and presentation.

9. Serve the Garlic Parmesan Zoodles hot as a flavorful and low-carb side dish or as a light main course.

Black Bean, Mushroom And Avocado Breakfast Scramble

INGREDIENTS:

- 1 small avocado, peeled, pitted, diced

- ½ cup onion, diced

- 2 small cloves garlic, finely minced

- ½ cup canned or cooked black beans, rinsed

- 2 tablespoons fresh cilantro, chopped (optional)

- 4 teaspoons oil

- 2 cups white button mushrooms, sliced

- 4 large eggs, whisked

- Freshly ground pepper to taste

- Salt to taste

Directions:

1. Place a skillet over medium heat. Add oil. When the oil is heated, add onions and mushrooms and sauté until soft.

2. Add garlic and sauté until fragrant. Add beans, salt and pepper. Pour eggs over it. Keep stirring until the eggs are set.

3. Divide into 2 plates. Place avocado slices on top. Garnish with cilantro and serve.

Blueberry Popovers With Berry Salad

INGREDIENTS:

For blueberry popovers:

- ½ cup 1%coconut milk

- ½ tablespoon stevia

- A pinch salt

- 1 egg

- ¼ cup blueberries

- ½ cup all-purpose flour

- ½ teaspoon stevia

- Cooking spray

For berry salad:

- ½ cup raspberries

- ½ cup strawberries, hulled, cut into thick slices

- ½ cup blueberries

- 1 teaspoon sugar

Directions:

1. To make blueberry popovers: Grease 4 muffin cups with cooking spray and set aside.

2. Add flour, salt and sugar into a bowl. Make a cavity in the mixture and crack the egg into it. Add milk and beat using a wire whisk until smooth.

3. Pour the batter into the prepared muffin cups. Fill up to 2/3. Sprinkle a few blueberries is each.

4. Bake in a preheated oven at 425ºF for 25 -30 minutes or until golden brown on top.

5. Meanwhile make the berry salad as follows: Blend most of the raspberries and pass through a wire mesh strainer. Discard the seeds. Add the puree into a bowl.

6. Add rest of the INGREDIENTS: into the bowl and mix well.

7. When the popovers are ready, allow it to cool for 5 minutes. Run a knife around the edges of the popovers and remove it carefully.

8. Sprinkle icing sugar on it.

9. Serve warm with salad.

Frittata Florentine

INGREDIENTS:

- ¼ cup canned sweet corn

- 2-3 tablespoons parmesan cheese, grated (optional)

- 1 clove garlic, minced

- 1 plum tomato, chopped

- ½ red bell pepper, chopped

- 4 eggs, beaten

- 2 tablespoons red onion

- 2 teaspoons extra virgin olive oil

- ½ cup spinach or arugula, chopped

- Salt to taste

- Pepper to taste

Directions:

1. Place an ovenproof skillet over medium heat. Add oil. When the oil is heated, add onion and garlic and sauté until translucent.

2. Add tomatoes, spinach, corn and bell pepper. Cook for 2-3 minutes.

3. Whisk together eggs, salt and pepper into a bowl and pour over the vegetables in the skillet. Cook until the sides begin to set. Remove from heat.

4. Sprinkle cheese on it.

5. Transfer the skillet into a preheated oven.

6. Bake at 350ºF for 25 -30 minutes or until cheese melts and the eggs are set in the center.

Raisin Roll Delight

INGREDIENTS:

- 2 eggs

- 1 egg white

- ¾ cup of cold water

- 6 tablespoons of butter

- 1 ounce of raisins

- ¾ cup of vital wheat flour

Directions:

1. Preheat the oven to temperature of 400F. Have a large, nonstick metal cookie ready. Put water and butter in the saucepan.

2. Stir the mixture till butter is melted. Meanwhile, mix two flours and a pinch of salt in a separate bowl.

3. As soon as butter has melted, add the dry mix
    in it and stir the mixture with a wooden stick
    thoroughly.

4. The dough will become smooth within a few
    seconds. Keep stirring and then remove from
    heat after about 20 sec.

5. Now stir in the eggs in dough mixture, one by
    one.

6. The dough will become creamy without
    settling.

7. Now add the white of the egg. Consistency is
    important to check as it is crucial to make the
    best rolls.

8. Once all eggs have been added to mixture, stir
    in 1 ounce of raisins that will be taste
    amazing. Put spoonfuls of dough a cookie
    sheet and place them close together.

9. Now bake the rolls at 450F   for 15 minutes
    and check it till they become golden brown on
    top.

10. The rolls are ready. Freeze the rolls promptly
    that you plan to use later. You can also toast
    them but they toast much rapidly so use the
    lowest settings.

Sandwich Bread

INGREDIENTS:

- ½ sour cream
- 1 teaspoon baking powder
- 4 teaspoons olive oil
- 3 eggs
- ¼ ground flax seeds
- ¼ ground sesame seeds
- ¼ cup protein powder

Directions:

1. Preheat the oven to 350F. Mix all the INGREDIENTS: together and put them in a greased nonstick pan.
2. Bake for 20 minutes and your tasty bread is ready for you.

Avocado, Bacon, And Egg Mix

INGREDIENTS:

- 1 ripe avocado

- 2-3 pieces crumbled bacon

- 2 boiled eggs, chopped into chunks

- 1 small to medium tomato

- Tbsp lemon juice

Directions:

1. Mash avocado and eggs, and mix all other
    INGREDIENTS:.

<h1 style="text-align:center">Grilled Chicken Salad</h1>

INGREDIENTS:

- 2 small potatoes, skinned, boiled and chopped

- 12 olives (optional)

- 4 sliced radishes

- 2 tbsp. olive oil (extra virgin)

- 2 tbsp. lemon juice

- 1 grilled chicken breast, sliced

- 2 cups spring salad mix

- 2 hard-boiled eggs, sliced

- Salt

- Fresh ground black pepper

Directions:

1. Mix chicken, salad, eggs, potatoes, olives, and
    radishes.

2. Whisk vinaigrette throughout salad (olive oil,
    lemon juice). Season with salt and pepper.

Mexican Frittata

INGREDIENTS:

- 3 chopped onions

- 2 seeded and chopped jalapeno pepper

- 2 lbs. lean ground beef

- 2 grated sweet potato

- 5 chopped garlic cloves

- 3 Tbsp. chili powder

- 2 tsp. cumin seed

- 2 salsa

- 23 eggs

- 3 pinch salt

- 3 pinch black pepper

- 3 Tbsp. coconut oil

Directions:

1. To begin this recipe, turn on the oven and let it heat up to 365F. degrees.
2. While the oven is heating up, bring out a skillet and heat up the oil inside before adding in the jalapeno and the onions.
3. Let these 2 INGREDIENTS: saute until they become tender and then add in the ground beef and cook everything until the meat begins to brown.
4. Next, you can add in the garlic and the potato, continuing to cook so that the potato can become soft and the meat is thoroughly browned.
5. At this time you can add in the salsa, cumin, and chili powder, making sure to stir to combine and heat it all through, adding in pepper and salt as needed.
6. Transfer this mixture over to a baking dish.

7. Bring out a bowl and beat the eggs thoroughly
    before pouring them on top of the mixture
    inside the baking pan.

8. Cover the pan with some foil and place into
    the oven to bake for about 45 to 50 minutes.

9. After this time, take the foil off and bake until
    the center has time to set, which will take
    another 15 to 20 minutes.

10. Take the baking dish from the oven and allow
    it time to cool a bit before cutting and
    enjoying.

Double Cream Chocolate Fudge

INGREDIENTS:

- 55 g dark chocolate

- 9 x 12cm tray

- 445 ml double cream

- 55 g unsalted butter

- ½ tsp. vanilla extract

Directions:

1. Preparation tip! Place the double cream in a thick-based saucepan over moderate-high heat.

2. Stir the vanilla extract into the double cream and bring to a gentle boil.

3. Lower the heat.

4. Let simmer while stirring occasionally until the double cream has reduced to half the initial amount.

5. Incorporate the room temperature butter until you achieve a smooth batter.

6. Remove pan from heat and set aside.

7. Stir the chocolate into the hot mixture until completely melted and well combined.

8. Pour the batter into your ray. Place in the fridge for 2-2 ½ hours.

9. Remove tray from the fridge.

10. Use a fine strainer to sprinkle a uniform layer of cocoa powder on top.

11. Cut the chocolate fudge into 23 pieces and serve one piece as dessert!

Lemon Garlic Air Fryer Shrimp

INGREDIENTS:

- 2 cloves garlic, minced

- Juice of 1 lemon

- Salt and pepper, to taste

- 1 pound shrimp, peeled and deveined

- 2 tablespoons olive oil

- Chopped parsley, for garnish

Directions:

1. Preheat the air fryer to 400°F (200°C).

2. In a bowl, combine the shrimp, olive oil, minced garlic, lemon juice, salt, and pepper. Toss to coat the shrimp evenly.

3. Place the shrimp in a single layer in the air fryer basket.

4. Cook for 5-7 minutes, shaking the basket halfway through cooking, until the shrimp are pink and cooked through.

5. Garnish with chopped parsley and serve hot.

Italian Herb Air Fryer Chicken Thighs

INGREDIENTS:

- 1/2 teaspoon garlic powder

- 1/2 teaspoon onion powder

- Salt and pepper, to taste

- 4 chicken thighs, bone-in and skin-on

- 1 tablespoon olive oil

- 1 teaspoon dried Italian seasoning

- Fresh basil, for garnish

Directions:

1. Preheat the air fryer to 400°F (200°C).

2. Rub the chicken thighs with olive oil, dried Italian seasoning, garlic powder, onion powder, salt, and pepper.

3. Place the chicken thighs in the air fryer basket, skin-side down.

4. Cook for 12 minutes, then flip the chicken thighs and cook for an additional 10-12 minutes until the chicken is cooked through and the skin is crispy.

5. Garnish with fresh basil and serve hot.

Tuna Topped Pickles

INGREDIENTS:

- 1 can light flaked tuna, drained

- 5 dill pickles

- ¼ tsp pepper

- ¼ cup full-fat mayonnaise

Directions:

1. Slice pickles in half, lengthwise. With a spoon, deseed the pickles and discard seeds.
2. In a small bowl, mix well the mayo, dill, and tuna using a fork.
3. Evenly divide them into 10 and spread over deseeded pickles.
4. Garnish with more dill on top and sprinkle black pepper.
5. Evenly divide into suggested servings and enjoy.

Parsnip And Carrot Fries With Aioli

INGREDIENTS:

- 4 tbsp mayonnaise

- 2 garlic cloves, minced

- Salt and black pepper to taste

- 3 tbsp lemon juice

Parsnip and Carrots Fries:

- 6 medium parsnips, julienned

- 3 large carrots, julienned

- 2 tbsp olive oil

- 5 tbsp chopped parsley

- Salt and black pepper to taste

Directions:

1. Preheat the oven to 400ºF. Make the aioli by mixing the mayonnaise with garlic, salt, pepper, and lemon juice; then refrigerate for 30 minutes.

2. Spread the parsnip and carrots on a baking sheet.

3. Drizzle with olive oil, sprinkle with salt, and pepper, and rub the seasoning into the veggies. Bake for 35 minutes.

4. Remove and transfer to a plate. Garnish the vegetables with parsley and serve with the chilled aioli.

Chicken Cacciatore

INGREDIENTS:

- 7 bone-in, skin-on chicken thighs

- 2 yellow onion,

- sliced in half-moon slices with the grain

- 10 ounces mushrooms, sliced thin

- 7 cloves, coarsely chopped

- 2 bell pepper,

- cut into approximately 2-inch strips

- 1/2 teaspoon red pepper flakes

- 1/2 cup red wine, 28 ounces crushed tomatoes

- 3 tablespoons of tomato paste

- 2 teaspoon of dried oregano

- 3 teaspoons fresh rosemary, chopped

- 1/2 cup mixed pitted green olives and kalamata

- 2 teaspoon of capers, unrinsed

- 2 teaspoon of sea salt

- 1/2 teaspoon ground black pepper

- 3 tablespoons fresh parsley, roughly chopped

- a few fresh basil leaves

DIRECTIONS:

1. It's best to dry the chicken off before cooking. To taste, add salt and pepper. For a golden crust on the chicken, saute it in a tablespoon of olive oil for three minutes on each side over medium heat. Please take out the chicken and put it to the side.

2. For 3 minutes over medium heat, sauté the onions and mushrooms in the olive oil in the same pan.

3. Sauté for a further minute after adding the garlic, bell pepper, and red pepper flakes.

4. Reduce heat and stir in the wine, crushed tomatoes, tomato paste, herbs, salt, and pepper. Put everything together by stirring it well.

5. Add chicken that has been seared to the sauce. Simmer for 25 minutes. If you leave it uncovered, you may hear a little sputtering, but splatter screens are excellent.

6. Check the chicken's temperature; we want it to be 165 degrees Fahrenheit inside. When in doubt, simmer for longer.

7. Thighs with the bone in might take as long as 35 minutes.

8. The cookery time for weakling breasts is lessened to only 15 to 20 minutes.

9. Throw some fresh basil leaves on top and mix with some parsley. Top with cooked spaghetti

and creamy polenta, or savour with a slice of crusty bread.

Easy Roasted Turkey Legs

INGREDIENTS:

- 1 tbsp paprika

- 1 tbsp garlic powder

- 1 tsp dried oregano

- ½ tsp ground cumin

- 1 tsp salt

- Slices of lemon slices and red onion,

- some fresh rosemary and garlic cloves

- 3 large turkey legs

- 3 tbsp extra virgin olive oil

- 1/2 tsp pepper

Directions:

1. Set the temperature to 175 degrees Celsius. Spread red onion slices, lemon slices, rosemary, and garlic cloves on a lined roasting pan in an even layer.
2. Rub some olive oil on the turkey leg (both sides).
3. Incorporate the paprika, garlic powder, dried oregano, powdered cumin, salt, and pepper in a small glass bowl and stir to combine.
4. Season the turkey on both sides with the spice blend.
5. Toss the turkey leg, skin side down, with the sliced onions, lemons, rosemary, and garlic. Roast for 30 minutes. Cook the legs for an additional 30 minutes to an hour, skin side up, to reach an internal temperature of 165 degrees Fahrenheit.

6. Take the turkey out of the oven, surround it loosely with foil, and tolerate it seat for 20 minutes. Enjoy!

Keto Caesar Salad

INGREDIENTS:

- 1 clove of garlic, minced

- 1/4 teaspoon Dijon mustard

- Salt and pepper, to taste

- 1 head of romaine lettuce, washed and chopped 1/4 cup grated Parmesan cheese

- 2 tablespoons olive oil

- 2 tablespoons lemon juice

- Optional: diced cooked chicken, bacon bits, or croutons

Directions:

1. In a large bowl, combine the lettuce, Parmesan cheese, and any optional INGREDIENTS: (if using).

2. In a small bowl, whisk together the olive oil, lemon juice, garlic, mustard, salt, and pepper.

3. Pour the dressing over the salad and toss to combine.

4. Serve immediately and enjoy!

Keto-Friendly Hamburger

INGREDIENTS:

- 1 egg

- 2 tablespoons grated cheese (cheddar or feta)
  1 tablespoon olive oil or butter

- 1 lettuce leaf or 1 low-carb bun

- 1 lb. ground beef (80% lean, 20% fat) Salt and pepper, to taste

- 1/4 cup diced onion

- 1 clove of garlic, minced

- Optional: cheese, bacon, avocado, mayo, or any other keto-friendly toppings

Directions:

1. In a large bowl, combine the ground beef, salt, pepper, onion, garlic, egg, and cheese.
2. Mix everything well and form it into 4 patties.

3. Heat a non-stick skillet over medium-high heat and add the olive oil or butter.

4. Once the skillet is hot, add the patties and cook for 3-4 minutes per side, or until fully cooked.

5. Serve the burgers on a lettuce leaf or low-carb bun with any desired toppings. Enjoy!

Egg Omelets With Cheese, Mushrooms, And Spinach

INGREDIENTS:

- 1/2 cup of shredded cheese

- 1/2 cup of diced mushrooms

- 1/2 cup of fresh spinach leaves

- 3 large eggs

- 2 tablespoons of butter

- Salt and pepper to taste

Directions:

1. In a medium bowl, beat the eggs until frothy.

2. Heat the butter in a medium non-stick skillet over medium-high heat.

3. Pour the eggs into the skillet and cook, stirring occasionally, until the eggs are almost set.

4. Add the cheese, mushrooms, and spinach to the eggs, stirring until the cheese is melted and the vegetables are cooked through.

5. To taste, add salt and pepper to the food.

6. Fold the omelet in half and slide onto a plate. Serve warm. Enjoy!

Grilled Chicken Salad With Lettuce, Tomatoes, Avocado, And A Low-Carb Dressing

INGREDIENTS:

- Salt and pepper

- 2 cups of lettuce, chopped

- 2 tomatoes, diced

- 1 avocado, sliced

- 2 boneless and skinless chicken breasts

- 2 tablespoons of olive oil

- 2 tablespoons of low-carb salad dressing (e.g. balsamic vinaigrette)

Directions:

1. Heat a grill pan or outdoor grill over medium-high heat.

2. Olive oil and salt and pepper should be applied to the chicken breasts before cooking.

3. Grill the chicken for 4-5 minutes per side, until cooked through.

4. Remove the chicken from the grill and let cool.

5. Once cooled, slice the chicken into strips.

6. In a large bowl, combine the lettuce, tomatoes, avocado and chicken.

7. Drizzle the low-carb salad dressing over the salad and toss to combine.

8. Serve the salad immediately. Enjoy!

Egg And Veggie Muffins

INGREDIENTS:

- 1/4 cup diced onions

- 1/4 cup chopped spinach

- Salt and pepper to taste

- 4 large eggs

- 1/4 cup diced bell peppers (any color)

Directions:

1. Preheat the oven to 350°F (175°C) and grease a muffin tin.

2. In a bowl, crush the eggs and season with salt and pepper.

3. Add diced bell peppers, onions, and chopped spinach to the bowl and mix well.

4. Pour the egg mixture into the greased muffin tin, filling each cup about 3/4 full.

5. Bake for 15-20 minutes or until the egg muffins are fully cooked and slightly golden.

6. Allow them to cool barely before removing them from the muffin container.

7. Serve warm or refrigerate for later use.

Egg White Vegetable Scramble

INGREDIENTS:

- 1/4 cup diced tomatoes

- 1/4 cup chopped onions

- 1/4 cup sliced mushrooms

- Salt and pepper to taste

- 4 egg whites

- 1/4 cup chopped bell peppers

- Cooking spray

Directions:

1. Spray a non-stick skillet with cooking spray and place it over medium heat.

2. Add onions, peppers, mushrooms, and tomatoes to the pan. Saute until the vegetables are tender.

3. In a different bowl, mix the egg whites till bubbling.

4. Pour the egg whites over the sautéed vegetables in the skillet.

5. Cook, stirring occasionally, until the eggs are fully cooked.

6. Season with salt and pepper to taste.

7. Serve hot.

Baked Coconut Crusted Fish Fillets Recipe

INGREDIENTS:

- 1/2 cup breadcrumbs

- 1 teaspoon paprika

- 1/2 teaspoon garlic powder and ½ teaspoon black pepper

- 1/2 teaspoon salt

- 2 eggs, beaten

- 4 fish fillets (such as cod, tilapia, or halibut)

- 1 cup shredded coconut

- Cooking spray

Directions:

1. Preheat the oven to 425°F (220°C) and line a baking sheet with parchment paper.

2. Combine the shredded coconut,
    breadcrumbs, paprika, garlic powder, salt, and
    black pepper in a shallow dish.

3. Dip each fish fillet into the beaten eggs,
    allowing the excess to drip off.

4. Press the fish fillets into the coconut mixture,
    coating both sides evenly.

5. Place the coated fish fillets on the prepared
    baking sheet and lightly spray them with
    cooking spray.

6. Bake in the oven for about 12-15 minutes or
    until the fish is cooked and the crust is golden
    brown.

7. Serve hot with a side of lemon, your favorite
    sauce.

Stuffed Baked Squid Recipe

INGREDIENTS:

- 1/4 cup chopped sun-dried tomatoes, 1/4 teaspoon dried oregano

- 2 tablespoons olive oil

- 2 cloves garlic, minced, and 1/2 teaspoon paprika

- Salt and black pepper to taste

- Lemon wedges for serving

- 8 medium-sized squid tubes

- 1 cup cooked white rice

- 1/2 cup feta cheese, crumbled

- 1/4 cup chopped fresh herbs (such as parsley, dill, and mint)

Directions:

1. Preheat the oven to 375°F (190°C) and lightly grease a baking dish.

2. Combine the cooked rice, feta cheese, chopped herbs, sun-dried tomatoes, olive oil, minced garlic, paprika, dried oregano, salt, and black pepper in a bowl.

3. Carefully stuff each squid tube with the rice mixture and secure the openings with toothpicks.

4. Place the stuffed squid tubes in the greased baking dish and drizzle with olive oil.

5. Bake in the preheated oven for about 25-30 minutes or until the squid is tender and the filling is heated.

6. Remove the toothpicks before serving. Garnish with fresh herbs and serve hot with lemon wedges.

Taco Stuffed Tomatoes

INGREDIENTS:

- 1 large onion (chopped)

- 4 large tomatoes (ripened)

- ¼ cup of sour cream

- ½ cup of lettuce (shredded)

- 1 oz. of taco seasoning

- ½ cup of Mexican cheese (shredded)

- 1 tablespoon of olive oil

- ¾ lb. of beef (grounded)

Directions:

1. Place a pan over medium heat and add olive oil. Allow the oil to heat up.

2. Add the diced onion to the pan and sauté for
    about 5 minutes until it becomes translucent
    and lightly browned.

3. Add the taco seasoning and ground beef to
    the pan. Cook for approximately 8 minutes, or
    until the pink color of the beef disappears and
    it is fully cooked. Strain any excess fat from
    the pan.

4. Prepare the tomatoes by cutting off the stem
    side and slicing them into 6 wedges, being
    careful not to cut all the way through the
    tomato. Repeat this procedure with all of the
    tomatoes.

5. Fill each tomato with the cooked beef filling,
    distributing it evenly among the wedges.

6. Top the stuffed tomatoes with shredded
    lettuce, shredded cheese, and a dollop of sour
    cream or Mexican crema.

7. Serve the Taco Stuffed Tomatoes as a
    delicious and flavorful appetizer or light meal.

Meatballs With Tomato Sauce

INGREDIENTS:

- 2 cups of tomatoes

- ½ cup of mozzarella cheese (shredded)

- 1 clove of garlic (diced)

- 2 tablespoons of parsley (chopped)

- 2 tablespoons olive oil

- 1 teaspoon of kosher salt

- 1 onion (chopped)

- 1 large egg

- ¼ cup of parmesan cheese, plus for garnishing, (grated)

- ½ teaspoons of black pepper powder

- 28 oz. of oregano

- Kosher salt

- 1 lb. of beef (grounded)

Directions:

1. Place a pan over medium heat and add olive oil. Let the oil heat up.

2. In a mixing bowl, combine the ground beef, grated Parmesan cheese, egg, salt, black pepper, chopped parsley, and shredded mozzarella cheese.

3. Mix well until all the INGREDIENTS: are evenly combined.

4. Form the mixture into approximately 16 meatballs of equal size.

5. Add the meatballs to the heated pan with olive oil. Cook them until they turn golden brown on all sides, rotating them occasionally for even cooking.

6. This should take about 8-10 minutes. Once cooked, remove the meatballs from the pan

and place them on a plate lined with paper towels to absorb any excess oil.

7. In the same pan, add diced onion and cook for about 5 minutes until it becomes translucent and lightly browned. Add the minced garlic and cook for an additional 1 minute until fragrant.

8. Stir in the dried oregano, diced tomatoes (including their juice), salt, and black pepper. Let the mixture simmer for about 10 minutes, allowing the flavors to meld together.

9. Return the cooked meatballs to the pan with the tomato sauce. Reduce the heat to low and let the meatballs simmer in the sauce for an additional 15 minutes.

10. This will allow the flavors to further infuse and the meatballs to soak up the sauce.

11. Serve the Low Carb Meatballs with Tomato Sauce hot, garnished with grated Parmesan cheese.

Fresh Fruit Muesli

INGREDIENTS:

- ¼ cup pomegranate seeds or blueberries to garnish

- 6 tablespoons rolled oats

- ¼ cup almonds, slivered

- 1 peach or nectarine, pitted, chopped + extra to garnish

- ¼ cup bulgur

- 1 tablespoon sunflower kernels

- 1 green apple, cored, grated

- ½ passion fruit

- ½ teaspoon pure almond extract

Directions:

1. Soak bulgur in a bowl of water. Cover and set aside for 30 minutes. Drain and place it in a large bowl.

2. Pass the pulp of the passion fruit through a wire mesh strainer. Press the pulp well with the back of a spoon. Add the strained juice into the bowl of bulgur.

3. Add rest of the INGREDIENTS: and fold gently.

4. Cover and chill until use.

5. Garnish with blueberries and peach and serve.

Onion & Chive Cauliflower Hash Browns

INGREDIENTS:

- 1 tablespoons green bell pepper, finely chopped

- Freshly ground pepper to taste

- 4 teaspoons olive oil

- 2 small blocks onion and chive Cotswold cheese, grated

- 2 large eggs

- 4 cups cauliflower, grated to get rice like texture

- Salt to taste

- 1 small onion, finely chopped

- 1 tablespoon red bell pepper, finely chopped

Directions:

1. Add cauliflower, salt, pepper, eggs, green bell pepper and red bell pepper into a bowl and mix well.
2. Place a nonstick pan over medium high heat. Add olive oil and swirl the pan. When the oil is heated, spoon about ¼ the mixture on the pan and flatten it with the back of a spoon or a spatula.
3. Cook until the underside is golden brown. Flip sides and cook the other side.
4. Sprinkle cheese over it when you flip sides.
5. Repeat with the remaining mixture to make 3 more.
6. Serve hot.

Hot Cereal

INGREDIENTS:

- 2 tablespoon flax meal

- 2tbsp oat bran

- 1 packet splenda

- 2/3 cup water

- 1 tbsp maple extract

- Dash cinnamon

Directions:

1. Stir all these INGREDIENTS: together and put
    in microwave for 2 minutes. Your tasty
    breakfast is ready to serve you.

Almond Flour Pancakes

INGREDIENTS:

- ½ tbs baking powder

- 1 tbs cooking powder

- 1 packet splenda

- 5 tablespoons almond flour

- 1 tbs water

- 1tbs sour cream

Directions:

1. Mix all the mentioned INGREDIENTS:. Put the pancakes into pan and cook in medium heat until bubbles start appearing. Turn the mixture and cook for a few minutes.

Low Carb Pancakes

INGREDIENTS:

- 2 tbs baking powder

- Cinnamon and nutmeg

- ½ cup ricotta cheese

- ½ cup vanilla protein powder

- 2 tbs heavy cream

- 2 packets splenda

- 2 eggs

Directions:

1. Mix all INGREDIENTS: while adding water till a fairly thin consistency is achieved.

2. When pan becomes hot, spoon the batter and cook it till bubbles appear on one side.

3. Turn in; cook for few minutes and pancakes are ready.

Seared Tomatoes, Steak, & Eggs

INGREDIENTS:

- Kosher salt and pepper

- 4 medium tomatoes, halved

- 4 large eggs

- 1 tbsp olive oil

- 1lb flanks steak

- 1 tbsp chopped fresh oregano

Directions:

1. Heat large skillet with olive oil medium-high heat. Season steak with salt and pepper. Cook steak, 4-5 minutes on both sides for medium rare.

2. Add tomatoes to skillet cook on cut side, until brown 2-3 minutes.

3. Separately, Crack eggs into nonstick skillet
    and cook 2-4 minutes

4. Combine eggs, steak, and tomatoes. Sprinkle
    with oregano, salt, and pepper.

Turkey Lettuce Wraps

INGREDIENTS:

- 1 tsp mayonnaise

- 1 tomato slice, halved

- 1 slice cooked bacon, chopped

- 1 romaine heart lettuce leaf

- 1 slice organic deli turkey

Directions:

1. Add layer of turkey, mayonnaise, tomato, and bacon on romaine leaf. Wrap and enjoy.

Fish Curry

INGREDIENTS:

- 3 can tomatoes

- Salt

- 5 Tbsp. canola or olive oil

- 5 chopped onions

- 5 sliced zucchini

- 45g. peeled and chopped ginger root

- 3 tsp. ground coriander

- 3 tsp. ground cumin

- 5 halibut fillets

- ½ tsp. turmeric

- ½ tsp. chili powder

Directions:

1. To start this recipe, you can heat up some oil in a pan or a skillet.
2. Once the oil is heated up you can place the onion inside and let it fry for about 1 to 5 minutes.
3. After this time you can add in the zucchinl and let it fry for an additional 1 to 5 minutes.
4. Next, you can take the ground cumin, ground coriander, chili powder, turmeric, garlic, and ginger and add them to the pan and fry for another 45 seconds before adding the fish into the dish and stirring it gently.
5. Add the salt and the tomatoes in as well.
6. Now you can cover the skillet and let all of the INGREDIENTS: simmer together for about 15 to 20 minutes so that the fish is able to be tender and everything is well heated.
7. When ready to serve you can garnish with some coriander leaf.

Fried Aborigines And Anchovies' Salad

INGREDIENTS:

- 390 g plum tomatoes (halved)

- 99 g anchovies in olive oil

- salt and pepper

- ½ lbs aborigines, sliced lengthwise

- tbsp. olive oil, for brushing

- 270 g mozzarella cheese

Directions:

1. Brush the eggplant slices with 10 tbsps. of olive oil on each side and season to taste.

2. Heat a medium-sized frying pan over moderate heat.

3. Add the eggplant slices and fry for 5 to 10 minutes on every side

4. while turning occasionally.

5. Remove from heat.

6. In a small bowl, mix olive oil with the garlic, lemon juice, and parsley until well combined.

7. On a serving platter to fit all eggplant slices, pour the garlicky dressing.

8. Arrange the aubergine slices on the dressing and allow 1 to 5 minute to absorb the dressing.

9. Flip the aubergine slices.

10. Add the tomato halves, anchovies, and cubed mozzarella over the aubergine slices.

11. Drizzle with lemon juice and the remaining olive oil from the anchovies and season to taste!

Coconut Curry Air Fryer Tofu

INGREDIENTS:

- 1/2 teaspoon cumin

- 1/4 teaspoon cayenne pepper (optional)

- Salt, to taste

- 1 (14-ounce) block of tofu, pressed and cut into cubes

- 2 tablespoons coconut oil

- 2 tablespoons curry powder

- 1/2 teaspoon turmeric

- Chopped cilantro, for garnish

Directions:

1. Preheat the air fryer to 400°F (200°C).

2. In a bowl, combine the coconut oil, curry powder, turmeric, cumin, cayenne pepper (if using), and salt. Mix well.

3. Add the tofu cubes to the bowl and toss to coat the tofu in the spice mixture.

4. Place the tofu cubes in a single layer in the air fryer basket.

5. Cook for 15-20 minutes, shaking the basket occasionally, until the tofu is crispy and golden brown.

6. Garnish with chopped cilantro and serve with rice or vegetables.

Bbq Cauliflower Wings

INGREDIENTS:

- 1 teaspoon smoked paprika

- 1/2 teaspoon garlic powder

- 1/2 teaspoon onion powder

- 1/2 teaspoon salt

- 1/4 teaspoon black pepper

- 1 head cauliflower, cut into florets

- 1/2 cup whole wheat flour

- 1/2 cup unsweetened almond milk

- 1/2 cup barbecue sauce

Directions:

1. Preheat the air fryer to 400°F (200°C).

2. In a bowl, whisk together the whole wheat flour, almond milk, smoked paprika, garlic

powder, onion powder, salt, and black pepper to make a batter.

3. Dip each cauliflower floret into the batter, allowing any excess batter to drip off.

4. Place the coated cauliflower florets in the air fryer basket in a single layer.

5. Cook for 15-18 minutes, flipping the cauliflower halfway through cooking, until the coating is crispy and golden brown.

6. Remove from the air fryer and toss with barbecue sauce until well coated.

7. Serve hot as a tasty appetizer or side dish.

Herb Roasted Air Fryer Potatoes

INGREDIENTS:

- 1 teaspoon dried thyme

- 1 teaspoon dried oregano

- 1/2 teaspoon garlic powder

- Salt and pepper, to taste

- 4-5 medium-sized potatoes, diced into bite-sized pieces

- 2 tablespoons olive oil

- 1 teaspoon dried rosemary

- Chopped fresh parsley, for garnish

Directions:

1. Preheat the air fryer to 400°F (200°C).

2. In a bowl, combine the diced potatoes, olive oil, dried rosemary, dried thyme, dried oregano, garlic powder, salt, and pepper. Toss to coat the potatoes evenly.

3. Place the potatoes in the air fryer basket in a single layer.

4. Cook for 15-20 minutes, shaking the basket occasionally, until the potatoes are crispy and golden brown.

5. Garnish with chopped fresh parsley and serve
    hot as a side dish.

Basil Keto Crackers

INGREDIENTS:

- A pinch of cayenne pepper powder

- 1 clove of garlic, minced

- What you'll need from the store cupboard:

- Salt and pepper to taste

- 3 tablespoons oil

- 1 ¼ cups almond flour

- ½ teaspoon baking powder

- ¼ teaspoon dried basil powder

Directions:

1. Preheat oven to 350oF and lightly grease a cookie sheet with cooking spray.

2. Mix everything in a mixing bowl to create a dough.

3. Transfer the dough on a clean and flat
    working surface and spread out until 2mm
    thick. Cut into squares.

4. Place gently in an even layer on the prepped
    cookie sheet. Cook for 10 minutes.

5. Cook in batches.

6. Serve and enjoy.

Garlic Flavored Kale Taters

INGREDIENTS:

- 2 tbsp almond milk

- 1 clove of garlic, minced

- 3 tablespoons oil

- 1/8 teaspoon black pepper

- 4 cups kale, rinsed and chopped

- 2 cups cauliflower florets, finely chopped

- cooking spray

Directions:

1. Heat oil in a large skillet and sauté the garlic for 2 minutes. Add the kale until it wilts. Transfer to a large bowl.

2. Add the almond milk. Season with pepper to taste.

3. Evenly divide into 4 and form patties.

4. Lightly grease a baking pan with cooking spray. Place patties on pan. Place pan on the top rack of the oven and broil on low for 6 minutes. Turnover patties and cook for another 4 minutes.

5. Serve and enjoy.

Buffalo Chicken Dip Recipe

INGREDIENTS:

- 1/2 cup Frank's Original Red Hot Sauce

- 8 oz block cream cheese, softened

- 1/2 cup sour cream

- 1/2 cup white Cheddar cheese freshly shredded

- 1/4 cup American cheddar freshly shredded

- 1/4 cup crumbled blue cheese

- 3 teaspoons green onions, sliced

- Celery sticks, carrot sticks,

- 2 tablespoon of unsalted butter

- 3 teaspoons of minced garlic

- 2 cups cooked chicken shredded

- tortilla chips, crusty bread pieces,

- potato chips for serving.

DIRECTIONS:

1. Prepare a 375°F (190°C) oven. Putting the rack in the centre of the range is the best bet.

2. Butter should be melted over medium heat in a cast-iron skillet of at least 8 inches in diameter. Throw in some chicken and spicy sauce, and let it cook until the sauce has thickened and decreased by half (about 2 minutes).

3. Put the heat on low and add the cream cheese, constantly stirring until it melts and is incorporated. Put an end to the cooking, mix the sour cream, and sprinkle over the two kinds of cheddar.

4. Roast until the cheese is melted and bubbling appears around the edges (about 10 minutes). Cook under the broiler (or on the grill) for

another minute to get a golden brown colour on top.

5. Use blue cheese and green onions as a garnish right away. Sticks of vegetables, chips, and croutons may be used as dipping accompaniments.

Paprika Chicken Drumsticks

INGREDIENTS:

- 11 chicken drumsticks

- 4 tablespoon olive oil

- 4 teaspoon paprika

- 2 cloves of crushed garlic

- the rind of 1 lemon

- salt

Directions:

1. Set the oven temperature to 200 °C (about 400 °F).

2. If you want to make cleanup simpler, but it isn't required, you may use baking paper to line a roasting pan.

3. Mix the marinade INGREDIENTS: (oil, paprika, garlic, lemon rind, and salt; you may use a

whisk or fork; the important thing is that you get everything thoroughly blended) and set aside.

4. I use a brush to apply a uniform coat of marinade on the drums after I've poured it over them.

5. After 40 minutes, baste the drums with the pan juices and switch to the grill for the remaining 5 minutes of baking if you like a crispier exterior.

6. Serve

Keto-Friendly Chicken Salad

INGREDIENTS:

- 1 tablespoon Dijon mustard

- 1 tablespoon lemon juice

- Salt and pepper, to taste

- 2 cups cooked and shredded chicken breast
  1/2 cup diced celery

- 1/4 cup diced red onion

- 1/4 cup mayonnaise

- Optional: diced apple, chopped nuts, or crumbled cheese

Directions:

1. In a large bowl, combine the shredded chicken, celery, red onion, mayonnaise, Dijon mustard, lemon juice, salt, and pepper.

2. Mix everything well and add any optional
   INGREDIENTS: (if using).

3. Serve the chicken salad on a bed of lettuce or
   as a sandwich.

4. Enjoy!

Keto-Friendly Spaghetti

INGREDIENTS:

- 1/4 cup chopped fresh basil

- 2 cloves of garlic, minced

- 1 spaghetti squash

- 1 tablespoon olive oil

- Salt and pepper, to taste

- 1/4 cup grated Parmesan cheese

- 2 tablespoons butter

Directions:

1. Preheat the oven to 375°F.

2. Cut the spaghetti squash in half lengthwise and remove the seeds.

3. Rub the inside of the squash with olive oil, salt, and pepper.

4. Place the squash halves on a baking sheet and roast in the oven for 40-45 minutes, or until tender.

5. Remove the squash from the oven and let it cool for a few minutes.

6. Use a fork to scrape the flesh of the squash, creating spaghetti-like strands.

7. In a skillet, heat the butter over medium heat. Add the garlic and sauté for 1-2 minutes, or until fragrant.

8. Add the spaghetti squash to the skillet, along with the Parmesan cheese and basil.

9. Toss everything together until heated through and well combined Serve and enjoy!

Turkey Lettuce Wraps With Cucumber, Carrot, And A Low-Carb Sauce

INGREDIENTS:

- 1 cucumber, thinly sliced

- 1 carrot, thinly sliced

- 1/4 cup low-carb sauce (e.g. teriyaki, BBQ, or honey-mustard)

- 2 cups cooked, shredded turkey

- 2 cups of leaves of lettuce (of your choice)

Directions:

1. Place the cooked, shredded turkey in a large bowl.

2. Add the sliced cucumber and carrot to the turkey and mix together.

3. Drizzle the low-carb sauce over the turkey mixture and mix until everything is evenly coated.

4. To assemble the wraps, place a large lettuce leaf on a plate and spoon a heaping tablespoon of the turkey mixture onto the center of the lettuce leaf.

5. Fold the sides of the lettuce leaf over the filling and roll up tightly.

6. Serve the wraps immediately and enjoy!

Beef Stir-Fry With Peppers, Onions, And Mushrooms In A Low-Carb Sauce

INGREDIENTS:

- 1/4 cup of low-carb soy sauce

- -1 teaspoon of grated fresh ginger

- Red pepper flakes, 1/2 tsp (optional)

- 2 tablespoons of sesame oil

- 2 tablespoons of rice vinegar

- 1 pound of lean beef, cut into thin strips

- 2 bell peppers, seeded and sliced

- 1 onion, sliced

- 1 cup of mushrooms, sliced

- 2 tablespoons of olive oil

- 1 teaspoon of garlic, minced

- 2 tablespoons of honey

Directions:

1. Over medium-high heat, warm the olive oil in a sizable skillet.
2. Add the beef strips and cook for 3-4 minutes, stirring occasionally.
3. Add the peppers, onions, and mushrooms to the skillet and cook for an additional 5 minutes, stirring occasionally.
4. In a small bowl, combine the soy sauce, garlic, ginger, red pepper flakes, sesame oil, rice vinegar, and honey.
5. Pour the sauce over the beef and vegetables and cook for an additional 5 minutes.
6. Serve hot over steamed rice or a bed of lettuce. Enjoy!

Scrambled Eggs With Cheese And A Side Of Bacon

INGREDIENTS:

- 1/4 cup of grated cheese

- Salt and pepper to taste

- 4 strips of bacon

- 2 large eggs

- 2 tablespoons of milk

- 1 tablespoon of butter

Directions:

1. Crack the eggs into a bowl and whisk them together with the milk until the mixture is light and fluffy.

2. Melt the butter in a medium non-stick skillet over medium-high heat.

3. Pour the egg mixture into the skillet and stir continuously with a spatula until the eggs are just beginning to set.

4. Sprinkle the cheese over the eggs and season with salt and pepper to taste.

5. Continue stirring and folding the eggs until they are set to your desired doneness.

6. Transfer the scrambled eggs to a plate and set aside.

7. In the same skillet, cook the bacon strips until they are crispy.

8. Serve the scrambled eggs with cheese, and a side of bacon. Enjoy!

Quinoa And Vegetable Breakfast Casserole

INGREDIENTS:

- 1/4 cup diced onions

- 4 eggs

- 1/4 cup low-fat milk

- 1/4 teaspoon garlic powder

- Salt and pepper to taste

- 1 cup cooked quinoa

- 1 cup chopped spinach

- 1/2 cup diced bell peppers

- 1/2 cup diced zucchini

- Cooking spray

Directions:

1. Preheat the oven to 350°F (175°C). Lightly lubricant a baking plate with a cooking drizzle.
2. In a large bowl, combine the cooked quinoa, spinach, bell peppers, zucchini, and onions.
3. In a separate bowl, whisk together the eggs, milk, garlic powder, salt, and pepper.
4. Pour the egg mixture over the quinoa and vegetable mixture. Stir until well combined.
5. Pour the mixture into the ready baking container.
6. Bake for twenty-five to thirty minutes or till the casserole is fixed and lightly golden.
7. Serving it warm.

Whole Wheat Pancakes

INGREDIENTS:

- 1 tablespoon honey or a natural sweetener of your choice

- 1 cup of low-fat milk

- 1 egg

- 1 cup whole wheat flour

- 1 tablespoon baking powder

- 1/2 teaspoon cinnamon

- Cooking spray

Directions:

1. In a mixing bowl, whisk together the whole wheat flour, baking powder, and cinnamon.

2. In a separate bowl, beat the egg and then add the honey and milk. Mix well.

3. Turn the wet INGREDIENTS: into the dry
    INGREDIENTS: and stir until it is mixed. Do not
    over-mix; a few wads are okay.

4. Heat a non-stick pan or griddle over medium
    warmness and gently coat it with cooking
    spray.

5. Pour 1/4 cup of batter into the pan for every
    pancake.

6. Cook till bubbles form on the feel of the
    pancake, then turn and cook for another
    minute or till golden brown.

7. Repeat with the last batter.

8. Serve with sugar-unfastened syrup or clean
    fruit.

Baked Stuffed Crab Shells **Recipe**

INGREDIENTS:

- 1/4 cup mayonnaise

- 1/4 cup chopped green onions and 1/2 cup chopped bell peppers

- 2 tablespoons chopped parsley

- 2 cloves garlic, minced, and 1/2 teaspoon paprika

- 1 teaspoon Old Bay seasoning

- Salt and black pepper to taste

- 12 crab shells (cleaned and cooked)

- 1 pound lump crab meat

- 1/2 cup breadcrumbs

- Lemon wedges for serving

Directions:

1. Preheat the oven to 375°F (190°C) and lightly grease a baking dish.
2. Combine the lump crab meat, breadcrumbs, mayonnaise, green onions, bell peppers, chopped parsley, minced garlic, Old Bay seasoning, paprika, salt, and black pepper in a bowl. Mix well to combine.
3. Stuff each crab shell generously with the crab mixture and place them in the greased baking dish.
4. Bake in the oven for 15-20 minutes or until the crab is heated and the tops are golden brown.
5. Remove from the oven and let them cool for a few minutes before serving.
6. Serve hot with lemon wedges for squeezing over the crab shells.

Roasted Moroccan Harass Spiced Salmon

Recipe

INGREDIENTS:

- 1/2 teaspoon ground paprika

- 1/2 teaspoon ground cinnamon

- Salt and black pepper to taste

- Lemon wedges for serving

- 4 salmon fillets

- 2 tablespoons Harissa paste

- 1 tablespoon olive oil

- 1 teaspoon ground cumin

- 1 teaspoon ground coriander

- Fresh cilantro for garnish

Directions:

1. Preheat the oven to 400°F (200°C) and line a baking sheet with parchment paper.

2. Mix the harissa paste, olive oil, ground cumin, coriander, paprika, cinnamon, salt, and black pepper to create a spice mixture.

3. Rub the spice mixture onto both sides of the salmon fillets, ensuring they are well coated.

4. Place the seasoned salmon fillets on the prepared baking sheet.

5. Roast in the oven for about 12-15 minutes. The salmon is cooked and flakes easily with a fork.

6. Remove from the oven and garnish with fresh cilantro. Serve hot with lemon wedges on the side.

Antipasto Stuffed Chicken

INGREDIENTS:

- 4 pcs of provolone cheese

- 1 cup of pepperoncini (chopped)

- Kosher salt

- Black pepper powder

- Parsley (chopped)

- ¼ cup of parmesan cheese (grated)

- ¼ lb. of deli ham

- ¼ cup of salami

- 1/3 cup of olives (chopped)

- 4 pcs of chicken breast (skinless and boneless)

- 2 tablespoons of olive oil

- 1 teaspoon of oregano (dried)

- ½ teaspoons of garlic powder

Directions:

1. Preheat the oven to 400°F (200°C).

2. Place the chicken breasts on a chopping board and make 5 incisions in each breast, making sure not to cut all the way through. This creates pockets for stuffing.

3. Grease the chicken breasts with olive oil and season them with salt, black pepper, garlic powder, and dried oregano, rubbing the seasonings all over the chicken.

4. Stuff each chicken breast with a combination of thinly sliced ham, salami slices, provolone cheese slices, pepperoncini peppers, sliced olives, and grated Parmesan cheese. Fill the incisions generously with the antipasto INGREDIENTS:.

5. Place the stuffed chicken breasts on a baking sheet, ensuring they are evenly spaced.

6. Bake in the preheated oven for approximately 25 minutes, or until the chicken is cooked through and reaches an internal temperature

of 165°F (74°C). Cooking times may vary depending on the thickness of the chicken breasts.

7. Once cooked, remove the chicken from the oven and let it rest for a few minutes.

8. Garnish the Antipasto Stuffed Chicken with fresh parsley for added color and freshness.

9. Serve the chicken breasts as a flavorful and protein-packed main dish.

Philly Cheese Steaks Lettuce Wraps

INGREDIENTS:

- 1 cup of provolone cheese (shredded)

- Kosher salt

- Black pepper powder

- 1 teaspoon of oregano (dried)

- 1 tablespoon of parsley (chopped)

- 1 onion (chopped)

- 2 bell peppers (sliced)

- 8 leaves of butter head lettuce

- 1 lb. of skirt steak (sliced)

- 2 tablespoons of olive oil

Directions:

1. Heat 1 tablespoon of olive oil in a pan over medium heat.

2. Add the thinly sliced onion, bell peppers, salt, pepper, and dried oregano to the pan. Cook for approximately 10 minutes, or until the vegetables are softened and slightly caramelized. Transfer the mixture to a bowl.

3. In the same pan, add the remaining tablespoon of olive oil. Heat it over medium heat.

4. Add the thinly sliced steak to the pan and season with salt and pepper. Cook for about 2 minutes, then flip the steak slices and cook for an additional 2 minutes, or until the steak is cooked to your desired level of doneness.

5. Return the onion and bell pepper mixture to the pan with the cooked steak. Toss everything together to combine the flavors.

6. Place provolone cheese slices on top of the steak and vegetable mixture in the pan. Cover

the pan with a lid and let it sit for 1 minute, or until the cheese melts and becomes gooey.

7. Prepare a plate and arrange lettuce leaves on it. The lettuce leaves will serve as the wraps for the Philly cheese steak filling.

8. Scoop about 1/4 cup of the steak and vegetable mixture onto each lettuce leaf, distributing it evenly.

9. Serve the Low Carb Philly Cheese steak Lettuce Wraps hot, garnished with fresh parsley for added color and freshness.

Cream Of Spinach Soup

INGREDIENTS:

- 2 teaspoons chicken soup powder

- 2 cups fresh spinach

- 1 tablespoon coconut oil

- ½ cup (38% fat) whipping cream

- 1 medium red onion, chopped into chunks

- ½ tablespoon tamari sauce

- 2 ½ cups water

Directions:

1. Place a skillet over medium heat. Add oil. When the oil is melted, add onions and sauté until translucent.

2. Add spinach and tamari and sauté until the spinach wilts. Add water and bring to the boil.

3. Add soup powder and stir constantly until it is well combined. Let it simmer for 5 minutes.

4. Remove from heat. Blend with an immersion blender until smooth.

5. Place the skillet back on low heat. Add cream and stir. When it is heated (do not boil), remove from heat.

6. Ladle into soup bowls and serve.

Poached Salmon Steaks With Horseradish And Chive Sauce

INGREDIENTS:

- 2 tablespoons onion, thinly sliced

- 1 small carrot, chopped

- 2 salmon steaks (4 ounces each)

- ¼ cup high fat sour cream

- 1 tablespoon fresh chives, chopped

- 1 cup 2% coconut milk

- 1 tablespoon lemon juice

- 1 stalk celery with leaves, chopped

- 2 black peppercorns

- 2 teaspoons bottled grated horseradish

- ¼ cup high fat mayonnaise

- Freshly ground pepper to taste

- ¾ cup water

Directions:

1. Place a nonstick pan over medium heat. Add milk, water, onion, celery, carrots and peppercorns and bring to the boil.

2. Lower heat and simmer for 7-8 minutes. Add salmon and lemon juice and stir. Cover with a lid.
3. Cook until the fish flakes easily when pierced with a fork. Remove from heat.
4. Remove the salmon with a slotted spoon and place on a plate lined with paper towels. Discard the liquid in the pan.
5. Meanwhile mix together sour cream, horseradish, chives, mayonnaise and pepper in a bowl. Set aside.
6. Place the salmon on 2 serving plates. Divide the horseradish mixture and place over the salmon.
7. Serve immediately.

Thai Dipping Sauce

INGREDIENTS:

- ¼ cup lemon juice

- Pinch crushed red pepper

- ½ tbs sesame oil

- 3 tbs fish sauce

- 1 tbs cilantro

- 1 tbs soy sauce

Directions:

1. Combine all the INGREDIENTS: and enjoy the delicious sauce with unusual fishy flavor.

2. It can be stored for months in a good cold temperature retaining its original taste.

3. However, other goods in fridge might get its smell. You must try it as this is something different.

Marinade

INGREDIENTS:

- 1/8 cup soy sauce

- 1/8 cup balsamic vinegar

- Ginger

- Garlic powder

- 4 shots Worcestershire

- 1/8 cup oil

Directions:

1. Mix all these INGREDIENTS: in a zip lock bag and then put chicken in the bag.
2. Marinate in refrigerator for up to 24 hours.
3. Turn the bag occasionally, not often. Since most of the marinade is not used, no carb counts are listed for it. However, it is

confirmed that the carbohydrate level is much

less as compared to regular sauces.

Apple Cinnamon Waffles

INGREDIENTS:

- 1 cup grated apple

- ¾ cup almond milk

- ¼ cup melted butter

- 1 tsp vanilla extract

- ½ tsp apple extract

- 1 ½ cup almond flour

- ½ cup flax seed meal

- 1/3 cup Swerve Sweetener

- ¼ cup unflavored whey protein

- 1 tbsp ground cinnamon

- 2 tsp baking powder

- 4 large eggs

Directions:

1. 1.Preheat waffle iron and grease

2. Mix, almond flour, flax seed meal, sweetener, whey protein powder, baking powder and cinnamon.

3. Stir in eggs, apple, almond milk, butter, vanilla extract and apple extract and stir until combined.

4. Pour mixture into waffle iron and close. Cook 4 to 6 minutes or until golden brown.

5. Remove Waffles and serve with sugar free syrup.

Mango Vanilla Smoothie

INGREDIENTS:

- 1 cup frozen mango

- ¼ cup plain Greek yogurt

- ¼ cup vanilla soymilk

- ½ tsp vanilla extract

Directions:

1. Combine INGREDIENTS: in a blender, mix until smooth. Pour in a glass and enjoy

Celery Sticks And Cream Cheese

INGREDIENTS:

- 2 tablespoons prepared horseradish, or more to taste

- 5 drops Tabasco or favorite hot sauce, or more to taste

- 1/2 teaspoon salt

- 1/4 teaspoon freshly ground pepper

- 1 bunch celery (2 1/2 pounds)

- ½ cup Cream Cheese (low fat)

Directions:

1. Separate the celery stalks. Rinse them free of grit, and peel to remove strings if desired. Cut the stalks into 3- to 4-inch pieces, leaving the tender inner stalks whole.

2. Wrap celery sticks in a damp cloth, and chill
    for 1 hour before serving.

3. In a small bowl, combine the cream cheese,
    horseradish, and Tabasco.

4. Season with the salt and pepper. Serve the
    cream cheese mixture with celery.

Creamy Curette Salad

INGREDIENTS:

- ½ cup pecans

- 5 curettes

- 3 tbsp. olive oil

- salt and pepper

- 215g rocket leaves

- finely chopped fresh chives

- 3 Romaine lettuce head

Dressing

- 3 garlic clove

- ½ tsp. salt

- ½ tsp chili powder

- 4 tbsp olive oil

- 345 ml mayonnaise

- 4 tsp. lemon juice

Directions:

1. Cut the courgette lengthwise.

2. Remove seeds and slice crosswise in 2 inch pieces.

3. Cut the romaine lettuce into bite-size pieces.

4. Add the zucchini pieces in a pan where the olive oil is shimmering over moderate heat.

5. Season to taste and allow the zucchini pieces to fry until golden.

6. Remove from heat.

7. In a salad bowl, place the rocket leaves, chopped lettuce, and chives.

8. Place the romaine, arugula and chives in a large bowl.

9. Add the sautéed courgette pieces and stir to combine.

10. Toast the pecans in the same pan as the courgette.

11. Season to taste.

12. Transfer into the salad bowl.

13. Mix dressing INGREDIENTS: until well combined.

14. Pour the mayo dressing over the courgette salad and toss to coat all INGREDIENTS: with the creamy dressing. Enjoy!

Chicken Tikka Masala

INGREDIENTS:

- 2 tsp. cumin

- 2 tsp. coriander

- 1 tsp. cinnamon

- 1 tsp. ground cardamom

- Masala Marinade

- ½ plain yogurt

- minced garlic clove

- ½ Tbsp. grated ginger

- Tbsp. lemon juice

- Lbs chicken thighs, skinless and boneless

Sauce

- Tbsp. olive oil

- 1 chopped yellow onion

- minced garlic clove

- tsp. minced ginger

- 1/6 tsp. ground turmeric

- 1/5 tsp. cayenne pepper

- Salt

- Pepper

- 5-5 ½ . strained tomatoes

- 3 tsp. honey

- ½ cashew cream

- 2 almond milk

- Tbsp. chopped cilantro

- 2 Tbsp. garam masala

- ½ tsp. chile powder

- ½ tsp. paprika

- Cayenne pepper

- tsp. salt

Directions:

1. To get started on this recipe, you will want to work on the Masala marinade.

2. To do this bring out a bowl and mix together all of the INGREDIENTS: until they are well combined.

3. Take the chicken and make a few slices in it before placing the chicken into a large bag. Pour the prepared marinade on top of it.

4. Seal the bag and place it into the fridge overnight or for two days before you complete the recipe.

5. The next day you can take the chicken out of the bag.

6. Use a paper towel in order to blot off any of the marinade that is still on the chicken.

7. Bring out a cookie sheet and place the chicken on it.

8. Place the cookie sheet under a prepared broiler for a 1 to 5 minutes so that it can become just cooked through with a 1 to 5 brown spots on it.

9. Depending on how big the chicken is, this could take 10 to 15 minutes.

10. Make sure to turn the cookie sheet around once about half way through the process.

11. After the time is up you can take the chicken out of the broiler and cut it into cubes.

12. Bringing out a stock pot you can heat up the olive oil inside before adding the ginger, garlic, and the onion.

13. Cook these until they begin to soften and are slightly browned, which can take about 10 to 15 minutes.

14. Add in the spices and stir for another minute before adding the honey and the tomatoes as well as seasoning with pepper and salt.

15. Partially cover up the pot and cook it over some medium heat so that the sauce has time to become thicker, which is going to take another 10 to 15 minutes.

16. Stir it a few times in order to prevent the sauce from sticking with the bottom of the pan.

17. At this time you can add in the cashew cream and the almond milk and then keep on cooking over a low heat for another 10 to 15 minutes or until done.

18. Add the chicken at the end and let the whole mixture simmer for just a bit longer so that the chicken has time to warm all the way back up.

19. Sprinkle the dish with some cilantro and serve the dish with some cauliflower rice if you would like.

20. If you need to reheat this dish to have at another time, just warm it up until it becomes heated through all of the way and enjoy.

Buffalo Chicken Lettuce Wraps

INGREDIENTS:

- 1 tablespoon lemon juice

- 1/2 teaspoon garlic powder

- Salt and pepper, to taste

- Lettuce leaves, for wrapping

- 2 cups cooked chicken breast, shredded

- 1/4 cup hot sauce

- 2 tablespoons Greek yogurt

- Sliced celery and carrot sticks, for serving

Directions:

1. In a bowl, combine the shredded chicken, hot sauce, Greek yogurt, lemon juice, garlic powder, salt, and pepper. Mix well to coat the chicken.
2. Preheat the air fryer to 400°F (200°C).
3. Place the chicken mixture in the air fryer basket.
4. Cook for 5-7 minutes, stirring occasionally, until the chicken is heated through.
5. Spoon the buffalo chicken mixture onto lettuce leaves and roll them up tightly.
6. Serve the lettuce wraps with sliced celery and carrot sticks on the side.

Parmesan Zucchini Chips

INGREDIENTS:

- 1/4 cup grated Parmesan cheese

- 1/2 teaspoon garlic powder

- 1/2 teaspoon dried basil

- 1/4 teaspoon paprika

- Salt and pepper, to taste

- 2 medium zucchinis, sliced into thin rounds

- 1/2 cup whole wheat breadcrumbs

- 1/4 cup egg whites (or beaten eggs)

Directions:

1. Preheat the air fryer to 375°F (190°C).

2. In a shallow bowl, combine the whole wheat breadcrumbs, grated Parmesan cheese, garlic powder, dried basil, paprika, salt, and pepper.

3. Dip each zucchini round into the egg whites, allowing any excess to drip off, then coat it in the breadcrumb mixture, pressing lightly to adhere.

4. Place the coated zucchini rounds in the air fryer basket in a single layer.

5. Cook for 10-12 minutes, flipping the zucchini halfway through cooking, until the chips are crispy and golden brown.

6. Remove from the air fryer and let cool slightly before serving.

Greek Style Air Fryer Lamb Chops

INGREDIENTS:

- 1/2 teaspoon dried thyme

- 1/2 teaspoon dried rosemary

- Juice of 1 lemon

- Salt and pepper, to taste

- 4 lamb chops

- 2 tablespoons olive oil

- 2 cloves garlic, minced

- 1 teaspoon dried oregano

- Fresh parsley, for garnish

Directions:

1. Preheat the air fryer to 400°F (200°C).

2. In a bowl, combine the olive oil, minced garlic, dried oregano, dried thyme, dried rosemary, lemon juice, salt, and pepper.

3. Rub the lamb chops with the mixture, making sure to coat them evenly.

4. Place the lamb chops in the air fryer basket.

5. Cook for 8-10 minutes for medium-rare, or longer for desired doneness, flipping the chops halfway through cooking.

6. Remove from the air fryer and let rest for a few minutes.

7. Garnish with fresh parsley and serve hot.

Perfect Roast Chicken

INGREDIENTS:

- 2 lemon halved

- 2 leader of garlic, cut in half crosswise

- 3 tablespoons (1/4 stick) butter, melted

- 2 large yellow onion, thickly sliced

- 5 carrots cut into 2-inch chunks

- 2 bulb of fennel tops was removed and cut into wedges

- 1 roasting chicken

- Kosher salt

- Freshly ground black pepper

- 2 large bunch of fresh thyme, plus 20 sprigs

- Olive oil

Directions

1. Make sure your oven is at 425 degrees F.

2. Take out the chicken brains. Be sure to wash
    the chicken well on both sides. You should
    trim the outside of any extra fat, pin the
    feathers, and pat it dry. Season the interior of
    the chicken generously with salt and pepper.

3. Put the whole thyme sprig, lemon halves, and
    all the garlic cloves within the cavity. Butter
    the chicken's outside, then season it once
    more with salt & pepper. Use kitchen twine to
    bind the chicken's legs together, then tuck the
    wings beneath its body. In a roasting pan,
    combine the onions, carrots, and fennel. Mix
    in 20 thyme sprigs, salt and pepper, and olive
    oil. Arrange in the bottom of a roasting pan
    and top with the chicken.

4. Chicken should be roasted for 1 1/2 hours or
    until fluids flow clear when you cut through
    the thickest part of the breast. Please take out

the chicken and veggies and place them on a
tray, covering them with aluminum foil. Place
the chicken slices on a dish and surround
them with the veggies.